Welsh Jol

A Little Book of Wonder ... vvit

Compiled by Hugh Morrison

Montpelier Publishing
London
MMXV

ISBN-13: 978-1511612241
ISBN-10: 151161224X

Published by Montpelier Publishing, London.
Printed by Amazon Createspace.

A tourist got on a bus in north Wales but was dismayed to find the bus failed to stop at the village where he was staying.

'Hey,' he said to the driver. 'Make sure you stop at the next village!'

The driver waved his arm and shouted back, 'Prestatyn!'

'I can't go all the way there,' said the tourist angrily. 'I want to stop at the next village.'

The bus driver stopped the bus, got up from his seat and pointed to the bell. He said loudly, slowly and clearly, 'If you want the bus to stop, PRESS. THAT. IN.'

*

Q. What do you call a Swedish pop group in Wales?
A. Aber.

*

Q. What does a junior Welsh civil servant call his superior officer?
A. 'Dad'.

*

First housewife: Blodwyn Pugh is getting married.

Second housewife: Married is it? Is she pregnant?

First housewife: No.

Second housewife: There's swank!

*

What do you call a Welshman who lives in an attic?
Evans Above.

Did you hear about the Welsh atheist who wanted to be converted?
They took him to the rugby ground and kicked him over the goalposts.

*

A loudmouthed tourist in a cafe was criticising the Welsh delicacies.

'Your Welsh Rabbit's got no rabbit in it,' he said to his wife, 'and this laver bread sure as hell ain't got no lava in it!'

'Pity,' said the waiter.

*

2,000 tiles bearing the letter 'W' have gone missing from the Scrabble factory in Bridgend. Police suspect vowel play.

*

A Welsh Assembly politician was being photographed for a newspaper interview. To make him look impressive, his secretary gave him a memo in Welsh to hold while he posed for the cameras.

The politician pretended to study the memo carefully until the photographer pointed out he was holding it upside down.

'Do you not think,' replied the politician angrily, 'that a man of my position cannot read Welsh any side up whatsoever?'

*

Did you hear about the Welshman who broke the world 100 metre record wearing mining boots?

He fell down the shaft.

Did you hear about the Englishman who met the Welsh mafia? They made him an offer he couldn't understand.

*

An English tourist was so fed up with the Welsh weather that he went to Dwyfor because he heard it was always dry there on Sundays.

*

Newsflash: A Welsh councillor has been accused of providing council jobs for nineteen of his relatives.

He has strongly denied this and pointed out that only eighteen members of his family were employed by the council.

His family have now proposed a vote of no confidence for missing one of them out.

*

An English politician tried gain access to the Welsh Assembly while a debate was going on.

'I can't let you in there,' said the security guard on the door.

'But look here,' spluttered the Englishman. 'I'm a cabinet minister.'

'I don't know what church that is, see, but I wouldn't let you in even if you was a Baptist minister,' replied the guard.

*

When you can see the coast of Devon from Swansea it is going to rain. When you can't, it is raining already.

The male voice choir was rehearsing for its performance of Handel's 'Messiah.'

'Very worried I am about the words of this piece by Mr Handel,' said Jones to the choirmaster.

'What's wrong with it?' replied the leader.

'Well,' replied Jones, pointing to the lyrics, 'it says here "Every valley shall be exalted, and every mountain and hill made low, the crooked straight, and the rough places plain." We can't be having that going on in Wales, mun!'

*

Some confusing Welsh phrases:

'I'll be there in a minute now'

'See those two houses on the hill? Mine;'s the one in the middle.'

'Whose boots are these shoes?'

'Hold these two sheep while I count them'

'And there it was – gone!'

'Throw the baby down the stairs its bottle'

'One day you'll come home lost!'

A Chinese restaurant opened in a small village in a remote part of Wales. The owner put up a sign in the window saying 'Special offer – Dim Sum'

Dai walked past the restaurant a few times and after a while he could contain his curiosity no longer. He went inside and spoke to the manager.

'Look you, I don't know what this 'sum' is, but if you haven't got any of it how's it on special offer?'

*

Landlord (to barman) I don't know where those football supporters over there are from, but they're throwing all the chairs out the window.

Barman: Wrexham?

Landlord: Well it doesn't do them much good!

*

A sheep farmer from England set up a farm in Llanfairpwllgwyngyllgogerychwyrndrobwllllantysiliogogogoch.

Sadly his sheep didn't survive the branding.

*

A Welsh minister called on the English couple that had just moved into the village. 'Will you be attending our chapel this Sunday?' he asked them.

The couple didn't want to go but didn't wish to appear rude.

'Well,' said the husband, 'We'd like to, but the service is in Welsh.'

'That's alright,' replied the clergyman. 'The collection is in English.'

*

BBC Newsflash: 'tonight's televised debate, "Is the BBC too Anglocentric?" will be broadcast live from the Welsh capital, Glasgow.'

*

David Lloyd Geoge's amours were notorious, though curiously not damaging to his career. During the Great War his daughter Megan was trying to jump a bread queue in Swansea.

'Who do you think you are?' cried the Welsh housewives.

'I'm Lloyd George's daughter', she said proudly, to which they all answered 'So are we.'

*

American tourist: Say buddy, what's the name of this place?

Local man: Rhosllanerchrugog.

American tourist: Gee, how do you spell *that*?

Local man: Just the way it sounds.

*

Welshman: I will now sing 'All Through the Night.'

Englishman: Couldn't you finish a bit earlier?

Three Welshmen in a pub praising the beer:

First Welshman: 'Best glass of beer I never tasted no better.'

Second Welshman: 'So did I neither.'

Third Welshman: 'Neither did I too.'

*

Newsflash: Details have come to light of a vegetable 'superfood' being secretly tested by the Welsh Assembly. It is thought to be a government leek.

*

'Yes', said the proud mother, 'our Evan is up in London learning pharmacy.'

'Well, he needn't have gone all that way,' replied her friend, 'he could have come to our farm to learn and welcome.'

*

Choirmaster: Evans, you've got it wrong again. I keep telling you, B Flat, B Flat!

Evans: I'm being as flat as I can, man!

*

'Oh Blodwyn, drinking makes you look so beautiful.'

'But I don't drink Dai!'

'I know, but I do.'

English tourist: How do I get to Llangollen?

Welsh farmer: Well, I wouldn't start from here.

*

Evans had failed to win a prize for his poetry in the Eisteddfod. Afterwards he got a spray can and wrote 'The judges are stupid twits' in big letters on a nearby wall. One of the judges saw what he was doing and, in a shocked voice, shouted out 'In Welsh, if you please, in Welsh!'

*

Patient: Doctor, I can't stop singing 'The Green, Green Grass of Home.'

Doctor: You've got Tom Jones Syndrome.

Patient: Is that common?

Doctor: It's not unusual.

*

Welsh antique shop owner (to new assistant): Don't call them jugs, Blodwyn, they are ewers.

Assistant: Oh, thank you Mrs Davies, and are all these basins mine too?

*

An English politician was giving a speech in Aberystwyth. He said: 'I was born an Englishman. I have been an Englishman all my life, and I will die an Englishman!'

'What's wrong, boyo?' shouted a voice from the crowd. 'Got no ambition, have you?'

*

Customer (in butcher's shop): Is this really Welsh lamb? It's got 'New Zealand' stamped on it.

Butcher: It may have been born in New Zealand but I can assure you it had Welsh parents.

*

A Welsh regiment was surrounded by Zulus. The soldiers fought desperately as the spears flew thick and fast. Young Private Evans stood up and began singing 'Men of Harlech' and more spears flew at them, killing Evans. Private Jones stood up and began to sing 'All Through the Night'. A spear cut him down instantly. Private Davies stood up and before he could open his mouth the officer shouted 'For God's sake man sing them something they like!'

*

Englishman: Is this the right road for Cardiff?

Welshman: Yes butt.

Englishman: But what?

*

Elton John sang 'Sorry seems to be the hardest word'.

He's clearly never been to Llanfairpwllgwyngyllgogerych-wyrndrobwllllantysiliogogogoch.

9

I once had a Welsh girlfriend with 36DDs. It was the longest surname I've ever seen.

*

My wife asked me if I was having an affair with a woman from Llanfairpwllgwyngyllgogerychwyrndrobwyllllatysiliogogogoch.

I said: 'How can you say such a thing?'

*

Item on a hotel bill in Cardiganshire: 'Wear and tear of mirror, 20p'.

*

A couple were sitting in their car in a traffic jam on the way to the Severn Bridge.

'I think the children in that car next to us must be Welsh,' said the wife.

'Why do you think that?' asked the husband.

'Well the windows have steamed up and one of the children has written something in Welsh with his finger.'

The husband looked and saw what had been written:

TALF SI ERYT RUOY.

*

Then there was the Welshman who was known as 'Jones the Piano'. The reason being, he would always cadge cigarettes off people, claiming that he'd left his 'at home on top of the piano'.

A foreign agent travelled to the valleys with orders to make contact with a Mr. Jones who lived in a small village. He was to identify himself give him the code message 'Auntie will be late for chapel.'
He didn't know the address so he knocked on the door of the first cottage he came to. The door was opened.

In heavily accented English the agent asked:

'Are you Mr. Jones?'

'I am.'

'Auntie will be late for chapel.'

Mr. Jones stared at him in confusion for a moment and then smiled.

'Ah, you've come to the wrong house. It's Jones the Spy you want!

*

English tourist: Where does this road go?

Welsh farmer: Up that hill.

*

A man arrived at a crowded pub in Swansea and couldn't find a seat.

He shouted out 'Mr Jones' house is on fire!'

Immediately there were fifteen vacant seats.

*

I've got the best wife in Wales. The other one's in England!

A certain political appointment once lay between a Welsh and a Scottish M.P.

An Englishman was asked who he thought should get the job.

'Well,' he replied, 'If we get the Scotsman we'll keep the Sabbath and anything else he can lay his hands on. If we get the Welshman he'll pray on his knees on Sundays and on his neighbours the rest of the week.'

*

Planning officer (to farmer): What are you building?

Farmer: If I can sell it, it's a traditional Welsh cottage. If I can't, it's a cow shed.

*

A Welshman, a Scotsman and an Englishman are out in the hills when they come across an old lantern. Out pops a genie and grants them one wish each.

The Scotsman says 'I want my country to be independent.' 'Whoosh', it was.

The Englishman said 'In that case I want my country to be surrounded by a big wall, to keep out the Scots, the Welsh and the French. 'Whoosh', it was.

The Welshman thought for a moment and addressed the genie. 'This wall around England - tell me more about it.'

The genie replied, 'It surrounds the whole country, is built of solid concrete and is 200 feet high, and utterly impregnable.'

The Welshman made his wish. 'Fill it with water.'

Evans was in London having an eye test. The top lines of the chart bore the letters:

C W M T W R C H
I S A F

'Can you read it?' asked the optician.

'Read it man?!' replied Evans. 'I used to live there!'

*

The villagers were admiring Farmer Jones' bumper crop of leeks. It was the biggest harvest anyone had seen in living memory.

Farmer Jones however was not happy. 'It will wear out the soil terribly,' he sighed.

*

An English motorist stopped at a traffic light on a lonely Welsh country road one foggy night and heard a voice outside in the dark.

'Any chance of a lift, man?'

With slight trepidation, the Englishman called out, 'Who's there?'

'Dai Gwyllym Lloyd-George ap Tegwyn ap Roberts' came the reply.

'I can't possibly take you,' shouted the motorist as he drove off. 'This is only a two seater.'

*

When the Roman legions were attacking Wales, they were set upon by one brave Welsh warrior with a club.

Eventually, with hundreds of men at their disposal, they managed to force him to retreat into a nearby cave.

They followed him in before running out, bleeding and screaming:

'It's a trap! There's two of them!'

*

The owner of a kebab shop in central Cardiff was giving an interview to a reporter. 'Owning this business has made me what I am today – teetotal and vegetarian.'

*

A Welsh geologist has claimed that Wales is bigger than England because of its hills. If Wales were rolled out as flat as England, it would be the bigger country of the two.

*

Two women from Cardiff were on holiday in Florida. A local man struck up a conversation with them on the beach.

'I love your accents,' he said. 'So, are you two girls from Scotland?'

'Wales, you idiot!' said the women.

'I'm sorry,' said the American. 'So are you two whales from Scotland?'

*

Father (to small son) No you can't have a stick of Llanfairpwllgwyngyllgogerychwyrndrobwllllantysiliogogogoch rock – you can have one in Rhyl.

*

Dai had been injured playing rugby so he went to the doctor.

'Doctor,' he said, 'every time I touch my back, my leg, my arm and my chest it hurts. What's wrong with me?'

The doctor examined him and said 'You've broken your finger.'

*

Newsflash: A Cardiff man was so overcome with patriotism on St David's Day that he had to be admitted to hospital after swallowing a daffodil bulb. Doctors say he'll be out in the spring.

*

Three Englishman walked into a pub and saw a Welshman sitting alone at a table.

One fellow said to the others, 'Let's pick a fight with that Welshman over there.'

His partner replied, 'Wait, we don't want to be arrested. Let's make him start the fight.'

The third Englishman said, 'Wait here chaps. I know how to do it.' He went over to the Welshman and said, 'St David was a flippin' sissy.'

To this the Welshman replied, 'Ah well you don't say!' and calmly resumed drinking his beer.

The second Englishman tried his luck and said to the Welshman, 'St David was a stupid fool that wore a dress!'

The Welshman again replied, 'You're very sharp, you don't say!' and calmly resumed drinking his beer.

The last Englishman told his friends he knew how to rile the Welshman and bounced up to the table and yelled, 'St David was an Englishman!'

The Welshman replied, calmly, 'That's what your mates were trying to tell me.'

Teacher: Can anyone tell me where Swansea is?

Little Johnny: Top of the second division.

*

A well spoken English gentleman sauntered into a pub in Llandrindod Wells and drawled, 'What's the quickest way to get to Brecon from here?'

The landlord answered, 'Are you walking or going by car?'

The Englishman answered, 'By car, of course, my man.'

'Well, that's the quickest way,' retorted the landlord smartly.

*

What does a Welshman have on his grave?

An epitaff.

*

It was 1925 and a man was standing in a pub in the Rhondda. His head was covered in scars and he wasn't a pretty sight. A young lad began sniggering and pointed the man out to his mates.

A big burly miner jumped up and grabbed the young lad. 'Never, never, make fun of that man. He's a hero, there was a big fall at Abercarn pit and he stood with a wooden bar on his head for 6 hours holding the roof up while his pals were rescued. That's why he bears those terrible scars.'

'Sorry, I didn't know,' said the young lad, 'But, how did he get that cauliflower ear?'

'Ah well, see, that happened when he was hammered into position.'

How many Welsh male voice choir members does it take to change a lightbulb?

None, they can't get up that high.

*

What does the station announcer say when the train arrives at Llanfairpwllgwyngyllgogerychwyrndrobwll-Llantysiliogogogoch?

'Anyone in there for here?'

*

Heard on a choir outing, 'Dai, you're too drunk to sing. You'll have to drive the coach!'

*

I live in London and people often say to me: 'You miss Wales?'

I say: 'No, I look nothing like her. She's got long blonde hair and wears a sash.'

*

What does a Welshman say when he puts a cigarette end in the bin?

'Tidy butt!'

*

During the controversy over the disestablishment of the Church of Wales the two chief protagonists were David Lloyd George and the Bishop of St. Asaph.

On one occasion Lloyd George addressed a meeting in a small Welsh village where he was introduced by one of the deacons of the local chapel as follows:

'We all know the remarks made on this subject last week by the Bishop of St. Asaph who, in my opinion, is the biggest liar in creation.

Fortunately we have here tonight Mr. David Lloyd George who will be more than a match for him.'

*

Swansea City are playing Cardiff City tomorrow and after all the threats of violence, the abusive language and the wild accusations, it'll be nice to get away from the wife and watch the game.

*

What do you call an Englishman holding a glass of champagne after a Six Nations game?

A waiter.

*

Caller: I'd like the number of the Argoed Fish Bar in Cardiff, please.

Operator: I'm sorry, there's no such listing. Are you sure you have the spelling correct?

Caller: Well, it used to be called the Bargoed Fish Bar but the B fell off.

*

An old Welsh miner in the valleys lay dying. The minister visited him and spoke about heaven.

'Do you expect to go there, minister?' asked the dying man.

'Yes,' replied the clergyman.

'And will you be an angel?'

'Yes.'

'With wings?'

'Yes.'

'And shall I also be an angel if I get to heaven?'

'Yes,' said the minister emphatically.

'Well then, I'll race you for a pound!'

*

Q. What does a Welshman use on his smartphone?

A. Ap.

*

A visitor to a small Welsh town which had four chapels, none of which were well attended, asked an elder of one dying congregation, 'How's your church getting on?' 'Not very well', he said, 'but, thank the Lord, the others are not doing any better.'

*

An Englishman visited Wales and wasn't impressed by the size of the mountains.

'What's so great about them?' he asked a local farmer. 'I could climb that one in a day,' he said, pointing to the rising peak ahead of him on the path.

'I don't know about that' responded the farmer, 'a young couple went up this path last year and never came back, see.'

The Englishman suddenly looked fearful. 'Oh! Did they die?'

'No,' was the reply, 'they went down the other side!'

A teacher asked each of the pupils in her class to write an essay about their holidays. Little Johnny described his trip to Aberystwyth, and surprised the teacher by spelling the town's name correctly every time he used it.

The next day the teacher asked him to the front of the class and said 'Show the class how well you can spell. Write "Aberystwyth" on the blackboard.'

'Please, miss, said Little Johnny, 'I can't any more – I've eaten all my rock.'

*

Minister: I see Jones the Beer died when his pub burnt down. His widow got a thousand pounds fire insurance.

Elder: There's a pity. He'll be needing that more where he is now.

*

A Welsh minister travelling home one night on the bus was greatly annoyed when a young man much the worse for drink came and sat next to him.

'Young man,' he declared, 'don't you realise you are on the road to perdition?'

'There's a pity,' replied the drunkard, 'I was trying to get to Penarth.'

*

American tourist (to Welsh farmer): 'Say, if we climb this mountain, how far will we be able to see? Cardiff?

'Further than that, look you.'

'London?'

'Oh, further than that.'

'Not Europe, surely?'

'Further than that, even, isn't it!'

'Say, look mister, just because we're Americans there's no need to make fun of us. Just how can we see further than Europe from the top of that mountain?'

The farmer smiled and replied: 'Well, see, by the time you've climbed to the top, you'll be able to see to the moon!'

*

Three Welsh ministers were discussing a recent religious revival in their town.

'It's been a good week,' said the Baptist minister. 'We gained four new members.'

'It's been good for us as well,' replied the Methodist minister. 'We gained six new converts. You can't possibly have had a better week than that,' he said to the minister of the Primitive Methodist chapel.

The Primitive Methodist replied 'Oh we've had a great week. I managed to get rid of ten of our real troublemakers.'

*

A Welsh farmer noticed a man on the other side of the valley drinking from a stream by cupping his hand in the water.

He shouted out in Welsh, 'Don't drink that, it's filthy!'

The man didn't appear to hear him, and carried on drinking.

The farmer ran over to him and shouted again in Welsh, 'Don't drink that, it's full of sheep poo!'

The man stood up and said in an upper class English voice, 'I'm terribly sorry old chap, I don't speak Welsh.'

The farmer paused and replied in English. 'I was just saying, use both hands, you'll drink more easily.'

*

English tourist: What's so great about Wales anyway? Take away your mountains, your lakes, your valleys and your rugby, and what are you left with?

Welshman: England.

*

Then there was the Welsh cloakroom attendant who said 'Whose coat is that jacket hanging up on the floor?'

*

Welsh Anglicans don't recognise the Pope.

Welsh Catholics don't recognise the Archbishop of Canterbury.

Welsh Methodists don't recognise each other in the off licence.

*

A Welsh preacher took as his text the parable of the five wise and five foolish virgins.

Having explained at length the meaning of the parable and the fundamental moral choice implicit in it, he ended his sermon with a fine peroration and asked his congregation

'And where would you rather be? With the wise virgins in the light ... or with the foolish virgins in the dark?'

*

BBC announcer: 'Wales covers an area roughly the size of Wales.'

The relationship between Wales and England is based on trust and understanding. The Welsh don't trust the English and the English don't understand the Welsh.

*

A farmer in one small Welsh village was regarded with some disfavour by the local chapel-goers because both he and his wife were heavy drinkers and indeed were known to drink beer out of the teapot.

However, they were induced to attend a frenzied revival meeting in the chapel and were so affected by this that both of them gave up their intemperate habits.

At the next meeting the farmer came forward to testify to the change in his life.

'Yes,' he declared, 'the Lord has converted me, has converted my wife and has converted the teapot.'

*

An American walked into a pub in a small Welsh village. One of the locals approached him. 'I haven't seen you round here before. Where are you from?'

'I'm from the greatest country in the world,' replied the American proudly.

'That's odd,' replied the local. 'You've a damned funny accent for a Welshman'.

*

What did the man from Barry Island say when he got pulled out to sea by a strong current?

'Tidey!'

A new road was being opened but at the last minute, the engineer realised there was no road sign to say it wouldn't be suitable for heavy goods vehicles. Quickly he painted a makeshift sign in English, but couldn't make it bilingual as he didn't know enough Welsh.

He asked the road workers but they were all Polish, so didn't know either. In desperation the engineer emailed the local council and asked for a translation. A few seconds later he got a reply, and carefully painted out the translation onto the sign.

The next day somebody complained to the council. 'Why have you got a Welsh sign on the new road saying 'The office is closed, we will reply to your email as soon as possible'?

*

Welsh film titles:

The Wizard of Oswestry
Trefforest Gump
Dai Another Day
Haverfordwest Was Won
Cool Hand Look-you
Dial M For Merthyr
The Bridge on the River Wye
Breakfast at Taffynys
Look Back in Bangor
A Fishguard Called Rhondda
Ammanford All Seasons
The Magnificent Severn
Borth of a Nation
Who Aberdares Wins
Nine and a Half Leeks
Our Man Fflint
Brokeback Mountain Ash
A Bridgend Too Far
Austin Powys
The Eagle has Llandudno

Mrs Jones (to husband) Evans next door is wanting to borrow your lawnmower.

Mr Jones: Borrowing our lawnmower is it? And on the Sabbath day too. Shameful. Tell him we haven't got one.

*

Q: What Welsh cheese must be eaten with caution?

A: Caerphilly.

*

A Welshman was shipwrecked at sea and stranded on a desert island. Five years later a passing ship saw him and when the crew landed they were amazed to see the island covered with buildings the Welshman had built himself.

He pointed out a house, a farm, a mill and two chapels.

'But what do you need the second chapel for?' asked the captain.

'Oh, that's the one I don't go to,' he replied.

Other books from Montpelier Publishing

Available from Amazon

Non-Corny Knock Knock Jokes: 150 super funny jokes for kids

A Little Book of Limericks: funny rhymes for all the family

A Little Book of Ripping Riddles and Confounding Conundrums

More Ripping Riddles and Confounding Conundrums

Riddles in Rhyme

A Little Book of Parlour Puzzles

The Bumper Book of Riddles, Puzzles and Rhymes

After Dinner Laughs: jokes and funny stories for speech makers

After Dinner Laughs 2: more jokes and funny stories for speech makers

Scottish Jokes: a Wee Book of Clean Caledonian Chuckles

Wedding Jokes: Hilarious Gags for your Best Man's Speech

Printed in Great Britain
by Amazon

33625674R00018

Woolly Bully

'Woolly Bully'
An original concept by Rebecca Colby
© Rebecca Colby 2022

Illustrated by Tamás Mayer

Published by MAVERICK ARTS PUBLISHING LTD
Studio 11, City Business Centre, 6 Brighton Road,
Horsham, West Sussex, RH13 5BB
© Maverick Arts Publishing Limited August 2022
+44 (0)1403 256941

A CIP catalogue record for this book is available at the British Library.

ISBN 978-1-84886-899-1

www.maverickbooks.co.uk

This book is rated as: Orange Band (Guided Reading)
It follows the requirements for Phase 5 phonics.
Most words are decodable, and any non-decodable words are familiar,
supported by the context and/or represented in the artwork.

Woolly
Bully

By Rebecca Colby

Illustrated by
Tamás Mayer

Woolly was a bully. He was big, bad, and hairy. And even a little scary!

No one wanted to be his friend.

When it was time to play, Woolly

wouldn't let Sloth join the games.

"You're too slow," he said to Sloth.

"No one wants you on their team."

Sloth hung his head and climbed

back up his tree.

When the game ended, Woolly picked

on Rhino.

"You smell funny," he said.

"Don't you ever wash?"

Rhino
lowered his
eyes and waddled
home for another bath.

When it was time for lunch, Woolly sat down by Bear. "You've got my favourite," he said, swiping Bear's food. "I love berries!"

Bear didn't dare stop Woolly. He kept quiet and ate the bits that Woolly dropped.

Woolly loved it when the other
animals did what he told them to do,
even though they often ran away
from him.

But one day, Woolly spotted an animal

who didn't run away from anyone.

It was Tiger!

Tiger snarled at Anteater. "Is that your tongue," he asked, "or a skipping rope?"

Anteater stuck his tongue back in his mouth as Tiger laughed at him.

Woolly couldn't believe his ears.

Tiger was cruel!

Later, Tiger growled at Antelope.

"Go away!" he said. "That's my spot."

Antelope jumped off the rock so Tiger
could curl up in the sun.

Woolly couldn't believe his eyes.

Tiger was mean!

Then Tiger turned on Woolly.

"What are you looking at?" he thundered.

"Stop it, or I'll throw you and your friends

into the mud!"

Woolly couldn't believe what was happening. Tiger was treating him badly, and he didn't like it.

Woolly looked to the other animals for

help, but they looked away.

They were too scared of him.

Woolly realised that he had been just as bad as Tiger. Now, he wished he had friends instead.

Woolly knew what he had to do
to make it up to the others.
He would save them.

He quickly moved closer to Tiger.

"Come and get me then!" he said.

Tiger bared his teeth and prepared to pounce. For the first time, Woolly didn't feel big, or bad, or scary. Just very, very scared!

"RUN!" he yelled to the other animals.

25

Woolly stood his ground and pushed back.

When the dust settled...

...it was Tiger who landed in the mud!

Woolly was never a bully again.

He was still big and hairy...

But he was also kind, and

everyone wanted to be

his friend!

Quiz

1. Woolly was big, bad and...
a) hungry
b) cuddly
c) hairy

2. What does Woolly do to the other animals?
a) He laughs with them
b) He bullies them
c) He runs away from them

3. Who scares Woolly?
a) Tiger
b) Bear
c) Anteater

4. Who falls in the mud?

a) Woolly

b) Tiger

c) Bear

5. What do the animals do at the end of the story?

a) They yell at Woolly

b) They bully Woolly

c) They become friends with Woolly

Turn over for answers

Book Bands for Guided Reading

The Institute of Education book banding system is a scale of colours that reflects the various levels of reading difficulty. The bands are assigned by taking into account the content, the language style, the layout and phonics. Word, phrase and sentence level work is also taken into consideration.

Maverick Early Readers are a bright, attractive range of books covering the pink to white bands. All of these books have been book banded for guided reading to the industry standard and edited by a leading educational consultant.

To view the whole Maverick Readers scheme, visit our website at www.maverickearlyreaders.com

Or scan the QR code above t view our scheme instantly!

Pink
Red
Yellow
Blue
Green
Orange
Turquoise
Purple
Gold
White

Quiz Answers: 1c, 2b, 3a, 4b, 5c